Original title:

Wristbands of Hope

Copyright © 2025 Creative Arts Management OÜ
All rights reserved.

Author: Maxwell Donovan
ISBN HARDBACK: 978-1-80586-159-1
ISBN PAPERBACK: 978-1-80586-631-2

Threads of Togetherness

In tangled yarn of colors bright,
We weave our dreams both day and night.
With laughter loud and quirks we share,
These threads unite us, everywhere.

A rainbow snuck from grandma's stash,
Each thread a joke, a silly clash.
A knot of friendship, tied with glee,
We wear our hearts, as you can see.

When one feels blue, the team will cheer,
A dance, a joke, a funny sneer.
In every twist, a story spun,
We laugh together; we are one!

So wear these threads, though they might fray,
Our bond's more strong than any play.
With goofy grins, we march along,
Threaded together, where we belong.

Celebrations of Connection

In silly hats and mismatched shoes,
We gather 'round to share our views.
A dance-off starts, with grace and flair,
Who knew our moves could cause a scare?

With giggles loud, we raise a glass,
To cheer each other, let's have a blast!
Connections formed in wacky ways,
A memory made that surely stays.

A prank or two, we plot with zest,
Our playful nature, we know best.
Through bumps and laughs, we find our song,
In this big family, we all belong.

So here's to all those bonds we make,
With joyful hearts in every break.
Each silly joke, a secret shared,
A celebration, for we have dared!

Chains of Compassion.

In a world of twisted fate,
We wear these links, oh so great.
They jingle, they jangle, with every move,
Silly reminders of love that grooves.

Laughter echoes, they're quite a sight,
Like a fashion choice gone very light.
Each chain a story, a giggle or two,
Bound together, we shimmer and hue.

Threads of Tomorrow.

Stitching futures with colorful thread,
Each twist and turn makes us feel wed.
We knit our dreams with a playful yarn,
Creating joy, like a garden of dawn.

With every loop, there's a silly cheer,
We tie them up tight, have no fear.
A tangled mess? Just part of the game,
In our fabric of life, they're never lame.

Ties That Bind Us.

Bungee cords of laughter, stretchy and bright,
They pull us together, oh what a sight!
With knots and bows, we dance and play,
Ties that bind us, in a funny way.

Each tug a giggle, a twist, a grin,
We wobble and tumble, let the fun begin.
Unraveling tales, as we hop and glide,
In this joyous bond, let's take pride.

Bands of Light.

Silly bands that glow, shining so bold,
They wrap around dreams, a sight to behold.
A rainbow of laughter, we wear them bright,
These bands are our giggles, lighting the night.

When we dance in circles, they sparkle and twirl,
Each bounce a reminder, let joy unfurl.
With every color, there's mischief and glee,
These bands of delight, oh so carefree!

Ties That Bind Us to Tomorrow

Twisted threads that make us grin,
Laughing through the thick and thin.
Like rubber bands around our dreams,
We bounce back, or so it seems.

Tangled up in joyful cheer,
We joke about our every fear.
Like silly string that flies about,
We tie our hopes, and twist them out.

Colors of Courage

Rainbow hues in every sway,
Each shade brightens up our day.
Daring hearts in vibrant bands,
Spreading smiles with fun-filled plans.

From sunny yellows to bold reds,
Laughter fills our silly heads.
In this color-coded spree,
We dance with joy, wild and free.

Strands of Faith

A mess of threads, no doubt it's true,
We stick together like glue.
With a wink and silly cheer,
Our hopes are strong when friends are near.

Knots may form and fray a bit,
But laughter's where we never quit.
In tangled joy, we find our way,
Holding tight, come what may.

Emblems of Endurance

We wear our badges with a grin,
Strap them on, and let the fun begin!
Life's a ride with ups and downs,
We chuckle loud, forget our frowns.

Each badge a tale, a giggle or two,
Like sticky notes in hues of blue.
In every stumble, we find our voice,
Together we laugh, we make a choice.

Hues of Happiness

In shades of pink, I dance with glee,
A splash of green, oh look at me!
Orange giggles come out to play,
While yellow beams chase clouds away.

With every color, a chuckle sounds,
Like jolly clowns in silly gowns.
When life gets tough, let hues unite,
For laughter blooms, a palette bright.

Sashes of Strength

I tie a sash around my waist,
With silly patterns, oh what a taste!
Each knot I tie, a little joke,
In the face of fears, I will not choke.

With polka dots and stripes that sway,
I strut around, come what may.
My sashes sing tales of grit and fun,
Turning battles into giggles won.

Allies in Adversity

In the wild of woes, we form a crew,
Dressed in laughter, it's quite the view!
We stumble, we fall, but always rise,
With playful pranks to brush off sighs.

Through chaos and clumsy, we find our way,
With friends beside us, come what may.
Our spirits high, we face the blight,
Turning struggles into sheer delight.

Banners of Belonging

Waving flags of quirky cheer,
We laugh out loud, casting aside fear.
With banners bright, together we shine,
In this wild parade, everything's fine.

Join the dance, don't be shy,
With mismatched socks, we reach for the sky.
Crafting joy in every thread,
With silly slogans, joy's widespread.

Threads of Unity

In the land where colors clash,
Folks wear threads that make a splash.
A pink for joy, a green for cheer,
They twirl around, spreading good vibes here.

A yellow dance, a blue parade,
Each thread a bond that won't fade.
With silly hats and ties askew,
They laugh and play, like kids anew.

Vows of the Heart

With knots so tight, they form a pact,
To share a laugh, to never slack.
These ties of fun, they link us all,
In goofy ways, we'll never fall.

With every twist, a story spins,
Of silly faces, and playful grins.
Together we stand, in colors bold,
A circus of friendship, never old.

Bridges of Belief

Across the river of doubt we tread,
With vibrant threads, we forge ahead.
No fear of heights, no time for gloom,
A rickety bridge, but plenty of room.

We dance along and laugh like fools,
Dressed in shades, breaking all the rules.
From one side to another, we cheer,
Building bridges of laughter, oh dear!

Weaving Wishes

In a garden where wishes grow,
We stitch our dreams, and off they go.
With each pluck of thread, a giggle bursts,
In bright patterns, it's laughter that thrusts.

Like kites that fly on a breeze so wild,
These whimsical wishes, forever child.
So let's weave tales, and dance all night,
With threads that twinkle in pure delight.

Armbands of Aspiration

In colors bright, they cheer us on,
With giggles loud, from dusk till dawn.
One size fits all, they promise glee,
Like rubber bands, they stretch with me.

They giggle when I trip and fall,
Remind me laughter conquers all.
With every twist and silly dance,
They keep my hopes in a tight prance.

Hues of Healing

In every shade, they're quite a sight,
A rainbow's dream in pure delight.
They mend the heart with cotton thread,
And bring back joy like freshly bred.

They wrap around, so snug and tight,
Providing cheer, a true delight.
When life gets rough, just take a peek,
And find the strength to laugh and speak.

Beacons of Bravery

Oh, what a scene, these bright delights,
They shine like stars on gloomy nights.
With every wish they catch the breeze,
And bring me luck like pots of cheese!

Each toss and turn, they twist and play,
Encourage me to seize the day.
When challenges seem far too steep,
These quirky bands help me to leap.

Cords of Commitment

In tangled knots, they hold us tight,
Remind us that life can be light.
With every twist, a promise made,
To laugh together in the shade.

They're playful ropes of friendship's call,
That guide us through and never fall.
With every tug, we join the fun,
These silly cords, our battle won.

Pulse of Possibility

In a world of rubber and cheerful bands,
We twist and turn with silly plans.
Colors bright, like a circus parade,
Wristy wonders that never fade.

Every bounce sends giggles high,
In our dreams, we learn to fly.
With every flick, a wish in tow,
Whispering tales of joy and glow.

Laughter bubbles, it's quite a dance,
With wristy wonders, we take a chance.
Wherever we go, our hopes are near,
In funky styles, we conquer fear.

Charms of Change

Strapped on bright, they jingle and jive,
Silly reminders that we're alive.
Shiny trinkets, each has its tale,
Our goofy dreams will surely prevail.

Every color a challenge to take,
With every slip, our hearts awake.
Funky designs, they twist and they shout,
With every step, we laugh out loud.

Beneath our sleeves, magic brews,
In mismatched colors, we choose our hues.
A wink of fate in every sway,
These charms of change guide our play.

Ankle Deep in Aspirations

With each step, we splash in dreams,
Ankles dipped in hopeful schemes.
Silly puddles filled with desire,
Jump in, jump out, the fun won't tire.

Sticky toes and laughs that soar,
In playful waves, we want much more.
With every skip, a wish we shout,
Aspirations loud, without a doubt.

We bounce along, each step a beat,
Silly movements, we can't be beat.
In puddles deep, our spirits gleam,
Ankle deep in the joy of a dream.

Future's Fabric

Tangled threads of colors bright,
We weave our hopes with pure delight.
Each stitch a smile, a giggle shared,
In this fabric, joy is declared.

Patterns wild, a blend of fun,
Our quirky dreams have just begun.
Laughter echoes, stitching tight,
In future's cloth, we shine so bright.

With every knot, a wish in tow,
Creating moments, watch 'em grow.
In vibrant spins, we dance and twirl,
This fabric of life, let's give it a whirl!

Threads of Tomorrow

In the drawer, they sit so tight,
Colors flashing, oh what a sight!
Little loops that bring us glee,
Hoping they hold destiny.

Twisting threads from left to right,
Tangled up in pure delight.
Riding high on dreams so bold,
With a sparkle of stories told.

Each tiny thread, a whispered cheer,
Resilient vibes, they bring us near.
In laughter's grip, we intertwine,
Threads of joy, they brightly shine.

So wear them proud, let spirits rise,
Even if they burn your thighs!
The future's fun in every hue,
Dancing stripes, we'll chase what's true!

Bracelets of Resilience

A stretchy band around my wrist,
Oh, how could I resist?
It works like magic, so they say,
It holds my less-than-okay day.

Dancing in my closet bright,
Loose threads cling to every plight.
With silly styles, they laugh and play,
Friends forever, come what may.

A carnival of colors leap,
Nothing heavy, nothing deep.
Wear them proudly, each unique,
Giggles echo, as we speak.

With every twist, a tickled grin,
We're warriors 'neath the skin!
A vibrant squad in goofy cheer,
Embracing joy, we persevere!

Echoes of Tomorrow's Promise

Rattling bands that sing of hope,
With tangled tales that help us cope.
In shiny hues, they shine so bright,
Whistling tunes to our delight.

Wiggle those arms, make them dance,
With each jingle, take a chance.
Voices echo from the past,
Telling tales that hold us fast.

Ode to giggles that brightly flare,
As friendship knots take us where.
Winding stories, rainbow dreams,
Chasing laughter, bursting seams.

In the future, we'll see the way,
Guided by colors that sway.
These cheerful bands will lead the thrill,
Together, we can bend our will!

Bands of Light in Shadows

In shadows deep, we strap and cling,
With silly bands that make us sing.
They glow like stars, they shine so bright,
Chasing away the looming night.

With every yank and cheerful snap,
We dance around the silly gap.
Strap 'em on for joy and glee,
These bands unite folks like you and me.

In rain or shine, we stand together,
Dancing in the stormy weather.
Every pop and every twist,
Can turn the frown into a fist!

So laugh aloud and wear them proud,
Creating smiles that speak aloud.
In every shade, we'll find our glow,
These light bands lead the way we go!

Markers of Motivation

On my wrist, a bright hue,
Squeezed tight by my middle shoe.
It gives a wink when I'm low,
Like a friend saying, 'Just go!'

Each color tells a big tale,
Of chocolate wins and balloon sails.
A rainbow packed with wild dreams,
And sneaky plans like ice cream themes.

When I trip on my own two feet,
It lifts me like a candy treat.
Though sometimes it twists my charm,
It's there, waving, to keep me calm.

So if you spot a rubber band,
Bouncing proud like a marching band.
Know it's not just for the style,
It's my giggle for every mile.

Bound by Belief

Tied tight on my wrist like a tune,
It dances in sun and the moon.
Each twist is a pledge, shiny and bright,
The world's a circus—I'm ready to fight.

With every flick, it jingles with cheer,
Pulling my dreams ever near.
It's my superpower, see me fly,
Like a pancake needing syrup, oh my!

In meetings when yawns reach their peak,
I give it a tug, a little squeak.
A nudge to revive my sleepy face,
While my thoughts race at a squirrel's pace.

So here's to the bands that hold tight,
With silly dances that feel just right.
Believe in magic, it's all a game,
Even if my wrist looks a bit lame!

Links of Love

On my wrist, a bling of delight,
A reminder to hug ever tight.
It mumbles sweet nothings of cheers,
While I face all my silly fears.

Each link is a giggle and glue,
Holding me close, like friends would do.
Connected and bustling, we prance,
In every flub, there's room to dance.

Those colors shimmy, they love to play,
Especially when I'm having a day.
Like a knock-knock joke, it's a laugh,
With each twist, I find the right path.

When life gets tricky, or a little rough,
This chain reminds me to be tough.
Bound by laughs and smiles they send,
In this fashion game, there's no end.

Woven Wishes

Threads of humor sewn around,
On my wrist, a joke profound.
Each twist a wish for a really good pie,
While my pet goldfish gives me the eye.

In colors bright like a frosty week,
Wishes tumble and mingle, they speak.
Like a robot with a silly dance,
Every spin is a playful chance.

Tangled in giggles, they twirl and weave,
Reminders to laugh and never grieve.
In every knot, a secret shared,
A promise of joy, be it dared.

So here's to the threads, snug and tight,
Woven wishes that feel just right.
A symphony of dreams, tied with care,
On my wrist, love's laughter fills the air.

Ties of Transformation

With colors bright and tales to tell,
They wrap my wrist, they cast a spell.
Each twist a laugh, a wink, a cheer,
Transforming fate, I'm grinning here!

Like magic threads in a jumbled game,
They hold the dreams, but not the blame.
When life gets sticky, just tie it tight,
With silly knots, we'll laugh in flight!

In meetings loud, I make my mark,
A rainbow flash, a quirky spark.
When stress arrives, I take a glance,
These charming ties make troubles dance!

So here's to threads that bring the fun,
Twisted joy, for everyone.
A fashion choice, or wisdom's blend,
With these ties, I transcend!

Patterns of Promise

Dancing dots and stripes galore,
They promise laughter, who's keeping score?
Each wrap a silly little jest,
A comfy hug, a trusty vest!

In meetings dull, they start to shine,
A patterned tale of a life divine.
With every flick, a giggle stirs,
Who needs fashion when fun occurs?

From polka dots to swirly waves,
They break the mold, no one enslaves.
In moments tense, they sway and swirl,
Bringing smiles like a playful twirl!

So here's to patterns, wild and free,
They promise joy, just wait and see.
With every tie, let spirits rise,
In every glance, a surprise!

Chains of Hope

These jolly links around my wrist,
Each one's a giggle, can't resist!
In silly shapes, they jingle and shake,
Creating joy for everyone's sake!

With each chain clasped, we unite,
A rollicking bond in pure delight.
They pull me up when I am down,
With shiny laughter, I wear my crown!

Metallic shine on days quite grim,
They add a sparkle, no chance to dim.
In stormy weather, they hold my hand,
Together we'll take a stand!

So here's to chains that dance and sway,
They lift the heart, come what may.
In every link, there's room to play,
Making magic, day by day!

Shields of Support

These colorful shields, my brilliant arm,
They guard my laughter, they keep me warm.
With every hue, a cheer displayed,
In storms of life, I'm not afraid!

Like quirky swords in playful fights,
They ward off gloom during silly nights.
Armored with fun, I face the grind,
With friends like these, peace I find!

Through ups and downs, they stand their ground,
In moments bleak, their joy resounds.
Each layer thick with cheerful might,
In every challenge, I take flight!

So here's to shields that always shine,
When life gets rough, they draw the line.
Together we dance, support in place,
With laughter's charm, we embrace!

Stitches of Support

In a world of thread and cheer,
We stitch our hopes, oh dear!
Beneath the fabric of our dreams,
We face the future with funny beams.

Each loop a laugh, each knot a jest,
A tapestry in which we invest.
We patch our fears with colors bright,
Dancing together in the warm sunlight.

Ribbons of Resolve

Ribbons tied in silly bows,
They wriggle like a worm that glows.
Tangled thoughts, oh what a sight,
Yet binding spirits, oh so bright.

With every twist a giggle grows,
Together we conquer our woes.
No frowns allowed, just silly grins,
Life's goofy dance, oh, it begins!

Fabric of Faith

Stitched together, piece by piece,
Our laughter weaves in a funny fleece.
With every patch comes a new tale,
A comedic journey on life's frail trail.

Threads of hope in vibrant hues,
Create a quilt that brightly woos.
We cuddle close when days get tough,
With comfort, fun, and warmth enough!

Insignias of Inspiration

Wearing badges of silly flair,
We prance around without a care.
Each emblem a wink, a playful poke,
In the game of life, we laugh and joke.

With quirky shapes, our joys collide,
A tapestry of laughs, we take in stride.
Inspiration found in every cheer,
Together we march, our path is clear!

Strands of Belief

On my wrist, I wear a thread,
It whispers tales of dreams instead.
A fashion statement, quite absurd,
Like a hopeful bird, just looking for a word.

Crafted knots that cheer and tease,
Each twist a laugh, such joyful ease.
My friends all laugh, they say I'm daft,
But in my heart, I've made a craft.

Colors clash, they don't quite match,
Yet in my mind, there's no scratch.
Each hue a giggle, each string a jest,
Oh, the hope hangs here, that's my quest.

So let them chortle, let them grin,
With every tug, I pull them in.
My wrist is lively, a playful sight,
A dance of joy, from day to night.

Echoes of Empowerment

When I bounce, it makes a sound,
Like someone's laughter all around.
These bands of cheer, they twist and twine,
A little jingle, oh so fine.

My wrist's a party, can't you see?
A colorful riot, just for me.
Each color glows, a wink, a nudge,
In the face of doubt, I give a judge.

People passing, they stop and stare,
What's that noise? Oh, we just don't care!
We wear our tales in bold display,
Life's a skit—we play all day.

So grab your thread and join the fun,
With laughter echoing, we've already won.
Together we twine, no frown in sight,
Chain of joy, forever bright.

Choices Woven in Time

Each band is a tale held close to heart,
With every twist, we're playing our part.
Funky designs, oh what a mess,
Choose your vibe, and feel the dress!

It's like a buffet, a smorgasbord,
Bright choices sprinkled, can't be ignored.
Pick your flavor, wear it with pride,
In the supermarket of dreams, we shall glide!

Doodles and sparkles, a zany parade,
Threads filled with laughter, never betrayed.
Hang tight to hope, let worries unwind,
In this playful circus, joy is aligned.

So come on now, don your best flair,
With smiles and quirks that dance in air.
Life's a canvas, and we're the brush,
In shades of fun, let's create a rush!

Tapestry of Dreams

Woven threads in vibrant hues,
A comic strip of life's good news.
On this loom, with laughter spun,
We craft our tales, all in good fun.

Each knot a giggle, every twist a cheer,
A whimsical dance with no fear.
Like silly string, we stretch and sway,
In the fabric of time, let's play away.

Beads of joy and trinkets rare,
A whimsical cosmos, light as air.
With every tug, we pull hope tight,
In this tapestry, the day feels bright.

So wear your colors, be bold and loud,
Join the parade, let's make us proud.
For each moment stitched is a treasure sweet,
In our quilt of laughter, life's complete.

Bracelets of Bravery

Once I wore a band too tight,
Thought I'd fly like a kite!
Instead I turned a funny shade,
And squeaked like an old arcade.

But every color caught my eye,
Promised me I'd learn to fly.
So with a laugh and silly grin,
I wrapped my wrist, let hope begin!

In stripes of pink and neon green,
I felt like an adventure machine!
If bravery comes wrapped like this,
Then count me in without a miss!

So dance around, wave your wrist,
Each one a giggle, can't resist.
With every twist, we make a scene,
Bold and bright, our spirits glean!

Colors of Conviction

Red for fire, blue for chill,
Wore them all for kicks, what a thrill!
With orange flair and yellow cheer,
I smiled wide, no hint of fear.

Some days they tangled in a mess,
Turned my outfit into a dress!
But who cares if it's all askew?
Fashion's fun when it's brand new.

Each hue a laugh, a story untold,
A rainbow spark, never gets old.
When colors clash, don't you know?
We dance to beats only we show!

So when in doubt, add some shade,
Let laughter come, let worries fade.
With every twist and turn we take,
We find our way, make no mistake!

Threads of Togetherness

Sewing threads with goofy glee,
Made a patchwork just for me!
Stitched a smile, put in a pun,
Wore it proudly, oh what fun!

Each thread a bond, bizarre yet bold,
Tales of laughter, I've been told.
One thread tickles, another glows,
In wacky patterns, friendship flows.

We tied them up with silly charms,
Caught in chaos, wrapped in arms.
With every tug, we're tight and free,
Stitched together, you and me!

In this tapestry, we find delight,
Creating joy, hearts feeling light.
With each new laugh and silly twist,
Together, we can't resist!

Chains of Change

Linked together in a silly chain,
Wobbling 'round, what's the gain?
Every jolt and every swing,
   Turns my life into a fling!

With every link, I laugh so loud,
   Join the party, join the crowd!
Who knew change could be so neat?
In clinks and clanks, we find our beat.

Each little jingle matches our joy,
   Like a kid with a flashy toy.
As we sway and rock with glee,
Change feels less like a big old spree!

So let us dance with each bold step,
Wear our chains, no need for prep.
In this groove, we'll find our way,
   Laughing loud, come what may!

Links of Light

In a world that's sometimes gray,
We wear colors bright and gay.
A stretch of plastic, oh so bold,
Each hue whispers stories untold.

When feeling down, we give a pull,
And laugh at fate, it's kind of dull.
With every twist, we start to dance,
These little links bring us a chance.

When life gets tough, we take a stroll,
In a rainbow, we find our role.
Strung together, a quirky crew,
Each clink and clatter, a hoot or two!

So wear your colors, bright and loud,
Join the silly, whimsical crowd.
With every laugh, bright bonds we forge,
In this circle of joy, let's all gorge!

Patterns of Perseverance

Through ups and downs, we trace our line,
With silly patterns, all divine.
Each turn and twist, a new escape,
A jester's hat or roller cape!

From polka dots to zigzag scenes,
Our fashion sense, a bit of beans.
In every fold, a tale to tell,
In laughter's grip, we all rebel.

We wear our quirks upon our sleeves,
With every giggle, the heart believes.
So, let us skip and hop about,
In silly socks, we twirl and shout!

These patterns hold, a stretch of cheer,
With every loop, we grow so near.
Come one, come all, let's join this spree,
Together we're as wacky as can be!

Tapestry of Trust

In stitches bright, our tales entwine,
A tapestry that's truly fine.
With every thread, a story's spun,
In laughter's light, we have our fun.

A knot of kinship, soft and tight,
In mishaps past, we find our light.
With every weave, we poke and prod,
Creating joy, a merry nod.

Each patch a memory, bright and bold,
A quilt of dreams, our hearts unfold.
So let us gather, stitch by stitch,
In laughter's warmth, we become rich!

We snip and sew, with grace and delight,
In this quilted world, we take flight.
With every hug, we seal our fate,
A tapestry of joy, it's never late!

Glimmers of Grace

In tiny glints, our spirits rise,
In every twinkle, surprise lies.
Like fireflies caught in the night,
With memories woven, oh so bright!

In gentle winks, the world waggles,
With every giggle, a smile haggles.
We dance like shadows, light on our feet,
In joyful chaos, life feels sweet.

With every flicker, we spin and sway,
In the grace of laughter, we'll play all day.
A sprinkle of joy, a dash of glee,
Together in this silly jubilee!

So let's collect these glimmers rare,
In every nook, spread love and care.
With each soft glow and glinting grace,
We find our joy in every place!

Emblems of Resilience

In a world so bright and bold,
We wear our charms like tales untold.
Plastic bands on every wrist,
Marking moments not to miss.

With every hue, a story's spun,
A laugh, a grin, oh what fun!
We strut about, a vibrant show,
In this parade of joy, we glow.

When life gets tough, we give a wink,
These silly bands help us not to sink.
They stretch like hope, they bounce back fast,
A comedy act, oh what a blast!

So when you see us, take a glance,
Join our quirky, silly dance.
For every laugh, a memory made,
Emblems of resilience, never to fade.

Colors of Courage

In shades of green and bright magenta,
We strut our colors like a great adventure.
Silly pop bands on our arms,
Turning heads with their quirky charms.

Orange for laughs, and blue for cheer,
Each color screams, 'We're pioneers!'
With glances sly and grins so wide,
We wear our hues like a joyful ride.

When moments seem to turn quite grim,
We wear our shades with a silly whim.
Courage may be fierce and bright,
But humor keeps our worries light.

So join the fun, let laughter flow,
With bands that tell what we all know:
Behind each smile, a story lives,
Colors of courage that joyfully gives!

Signals of Strength

A twist, a flick, a snap on skin,
These little bands, they always win.
A wave denotes we're doing great,
With laughter shared, and no debate.

Woven tales of resilience strong,
In silly moments, we belong.
Each color signals, 'Here we stand!'
Together, united, hand in hand.

When troubles loom and doubts appear,
Our bands jingle laughter, loud and clear.
Strength isn't always fierce and grand,
Sometimes it's silly, like a rubber band.

So wear them high, let spirits rise,
In each small band, a big surprise.
These signals shout, 'We are a team!'
In every laugh, we weave our dream.

Unity in Adversity

In the face of all that's tough,
We find the silly, we find the rough.
With bands that stretch and bands that glow,
We laugh together, come rain or snow.

When life throws pies and splats of goo,
We wear our shields, bright and true.
Silly symbols of our plight,
Join the fun, it's quite a sight!

Through all the ups, the downs, the twist,
In unity, we can't be missed.
We snap our bands with all our might,
In laughter's echo, we find our light.

So if you're down, come join the throng,
With silly bands, you can't go wrong.
In adversity, we find our cheer,
Unity in laughter, year by year!

Unity in Every Weave

In patterns bright, we tie our fate,
A twist, a turn, it's never late.
With laughter loud, we band together,
Our joy's a thread, no storm can sever.

Each color's choice, a bold display,
We dance in sync, come what may.
In every loop, a giggle waits,
As friendships bloom, we celebrate!

No gap too wide, no space too small,
With silly jokes, we stand up tall.
Like puzzles tossed in rainbow hues,
We weave our dreams, we cannot lose.

So here we stand, all side by side,
With silly struts, full of pride.
In every knot, we find a spark,
A woven cheer, bright through the dark.

Tokens of Tomorrow

With jingles bright, we make our mark,
A charm, a giggle, a little lark.
Each wrist adorned in colors bold,
A treasure map for tales untold.

In the joyous game of life we play,
Our dreams are silly, hip-hip-hooray!
From rainbow threads, we chase our fates,
And dance like ducks with silly gait.

These tokens wink with every twist,
A giggle fest, we can't resist.
In every hue, a promise sways,
For brighter nights and silly days.

With laughter loud, we skip along,
Through giggles, cheers, we find our song.
In bonds of joy, we all believe,
With humor stitched, we can achieve.

Beacons of Belief

In colors bright that shine so clear,
Each twist a tale, each knot a cheer.
We wear our fun through every thread,
A jester's cap upon our head.

These signals sent, no need for map,
With silly hats, and lots of clap.
In woven dreams, we find our way,
With funky moves, we laugh and sway.

Through every loop, a wink we share,
Life's silly dance, without a care.
In joy we trade, our smiles on show,
With laughter's light, we brightly glow.

So here's to bonds that lift us high,
With comedy, we soar and fly.
In every stitch, we find our place,
With playful hearts, we win the race.

Interwoven Dreams

In patterns bold we thread our wishes,
With giggles loud, and many fishes.
Each color sings a funny tune,
Beneath the sun, beneath the moon.

These twists and turns, a vibrant game,
Where laughter sparks, we fan the flame.
Our dreams are shaped with silly flair,
In every knot, we're free from care.

In every design, a spark ignites,
With jumps and jigs, we reach new heights.
Our hopes entwined, a merry dance,
In joy we twirl, and take a chance.

So here's our pledge, in hues so bright,
With every weave, we chase the light.
Our interwoven hopes will gleam,
As we all laugh, and chase the dream.

Stitched Stories

In a world of threads and cheer,
Colors dancing, bringing near.
They wrap around like hugs so tight,
In quirky patterns, pure delight.

Each stitch a tale, a laugh, a song,
Embroidered dreams where we belong.
With every twist, they twist the frown,
Brightening days in this bustling town.

A purple yarn for silly thoughts,
Orange dreams that cheer and rot.
Fuzzy feelings all around,
In fabric, true joy can be found.

So wear your colors, knot and weave,
Silly stories we believe.
In these threads, we find our spark,
Together shining, bright and stark.

Collective Courage

A band of friends, all tied in knots,
Each loop a joke that really spots.
Wearing colors, laughs collide,
With playful pride, we won't divide.

Bees buzzing yellow, blue like skies,
Underneath it all, a surprise.
They show the strength in silly ways,
Together laughing through our days.

They stretch and bend yet never break,
With every twist, new paths we make.
A rainbow's promise on our skin,
In every giggle, we all win.

So wear them bold and wear them bright,
With each adornment, hearts take flight.
In this wild dance, we find our groove,
With courage stitched, we learn to move.

Unity in Adornments

A riot of colors on our wrists,
Twirling laughter, can't resist.
Each design tells a funny tale,
From wild adventures to epic fails.

Stripes of mischief, dots of fun,
In this crazy race, we've all begun.
With every clasp, a bond so tight,
Adornments merry, spirits light.

They jingle, they jangle, in merry song,
Like a playful dance, we all belong.
With knots of joy, we take the chance,
To laugh together in this dance.

So join this chorus of color and cheer,
With each little charm, we draw near.
In vibrant hues, we find our way,
Together always, come what may.

Texture of Tomorrow

Frayed edges tell of whimsy days,
Woven dreams in colorful ways.
With each thread, a new delight,
Tomorrow's fabric feeling right.

Knotting laughter into time,
This bright array, a playful rhyme.
Textures of joy in every hue,
Binding us closer, me and you.

We strut around in our crafted pride,
With goofy grins, we don't hide.
Patterns clash, but hearts align,
In this silly space, we brightly shine.

So here's to tomorrow, let's embrace,
A tapestry of joy in every place.
With every twist, we weave our fate,
In laughter's fabric, we celebrate.

Symbols of Tomorrow

A bright hue on my wrist, oh what a sight,
It shines like a beacon, all day and night.
With every little glance, it wiggles and grins,
Whispering tales of the dreams that it spins.

When troubles come knocking, I simply just smile,
This colorful thread makes the tough times worthwhile.
It's silly and goofy, a companion so true,
Reminding me daily, I can start anew.

Just look at my accessories, a rainbow parade,
Each color a story, uniquely displayed.
If laughter's the goal, then this wrist is the key,
Unlocking the joy that's still waiting for me.

So here's to the future, a wacky delight,
With laughter and fun, let your hopes take flight.
These shimmering tokens are more than they seem,
They whisper of triumph, and chase every dream.

Chains of Compassion

On my wrist, a jingle, a clinky delight,
Each charm holds a story, oh what a sight!
They rattle and giggle, they cheer and they laugh,
Binding us all like a quirky art craft.

Friendship's a link that can never grow weak,
Silly little trinkets, they all seek to speak.
Each loop tells of laughter, each clasp a whole tale,
Together in mischief, we'll always prevail.

With every new bracelet, a giggle erupts,
Compassion's the glue that can never be trumped.
In times of despair, with a wink and a jest,
Our chains of connection will always be blessed.

So here's to the laughter, the bonds that we share,
These goofy connections will always be there.
With our colorful chains, let the friendships unite,
And dance in the joy of this colorful light.

Bands of Unity

A cuff of bright colors around my wrist bound,
In shades of the rainbow, my giddy joy found.
It wobbles and wiggles, a true buddy here,
It sends all my worries far out of my sphere.

When friends come together, we make quite a team,
With silly distractions that make our hearts beam.
These loops of connection, they wobble about,
Binding us closely, of that there's no doubt.

Each band tells a story, so quirky and fun,
Like mismatched socks in the bright summer sun.
Through giggles and grumbles, we lift up our kin,
A circle of laughter, let the fun times begin!

So wear them with pride, these bright bands we adore,
Together we'll conquer, there's always room for more.
With every new color, our spirits collide,
In this joyous parade, we are unified wide.

Tokens of Tenacity

With silly designs that jingle and jive,
These tokens remind me, yes, I'm alive!
Each twist and each turn holds a tale of its own,
Like a playlist of memories, all brightly shown.

When challenges strike, I just look at my wrist,
These trinkets turn stress into pure humor bliss.
Bouncing through troubles, they giggle and cheer,
A reminder of strength that's always sincere.

With colors exploding, my spirit ignites,
These tokens are magic in whimsical sights.
When life gets too serious, let laughter unfold,
With each little charm, I turn troubles to gold.

So here's to the laughter, the strength we all bear,
Each token a moment, a twist of the hair.
In the dance of resilience, with joy we persist,
Our quirky reminders, we simply can't miss.

Corded Connections

On my wrist, a rainbow spins,
Colors clash, like my old kin.
Each hue tells tales of days so bright,
Worn with pride, what a silly sight!

When I'm feeling low, I just tug tight,
It tickles my wrist, ignites delight.
Friends keep asking, "What's that for?"
I shrug and grin, then laugh some more!

They clink together, a jolly sound,
Like quirky bracelets that dance around.
Break out the snacks, we'll feast and cheer,
With these vibrant bands, there's nothing to fear!

So if you ponder what they're about,
Know they spark joy, without a doubt.
Let's tie them on, and frolic wide,
In this wristy world, we take in stride!

Emblems of Empathy

Strapped to my wrist, just like a badge,
A cluster of colors, oh what a fad!
They whisper tales of laughter and friends,
With each little band, the joy never ends.

Every time I wiggle, they jingle and peep,
A chorus of hopes that never will sleep.
Wear one for laughter, wear one for cheer,
With a flick of my wrist, all worries disappear!

They blend like a soup, odd flavors unite,
Brightly reminding me that all's alright.
A slap on my wrist, a giggle so free,
Empathy's bonds are the best kind, you see!

So if you spot them, don't judge too quick,
They hold all the quirks, and maybe a trick.
Fashion's great, but friendship's divine,
Let's tie some together, it'll all be fine!

Ties of Triumph

Twisty bands gathering dust on my shelf,
Each one a story, just like a self!
I sport them proudly, a colorful scene,
As I fumble for snacks, I'm quite the machine.

No medals for me, heck, I'm a champ,
These quirky ropes qualify for a stamp.
When life throws lemons, this is my fix,
I dance with these ties, pulling off some tricks!

Each tug's a reminder, I'm here to stay,
Like confetti at parties, all colors at play.
They sparkle and shine, with each little movement,
A goofy reminder of my life's improvement!

So grab your own bands, don't be shy,
We'll tie 'em up high, let our spirits fly!
In this circus of life, we're the stars of the show,
With ties of goodwill, we're never in woe!

Resilience Wrapped

On my wrist, a jumble of fate,
Each band a giggle, held snug and straight.
When the world gets cranky, it makes me grin,
I give 'em a twist, let the fun begin!

Oh please, don't take them as mere fashion,
They bounce with laughter, sweet and brash, in
Times of trouble, I pull on one tight,
As the world turns gloomy, I shimmer bright!

The colors they boast, a rainbow parade,
When friends all gather, our fears just fade.
We chuckle and joke, these ties we create,
In this fabric of life, we celebrate fate!

So when you're feeling down, just take a chance,
Wrap your spirit in colors, and join the dance!
With a flick of the wrist, let the laughter unfold,
In this merry-go-round, we shine tenfold!

Jewelry of Joy

In a world of bling and shine,
I wore a smile, oh so fine.
A bracelet made of rubber bands,
It promises joy from far-off lands.

Each color bright, a silly charm,
Some think it's style, for me, no harm.
They jingle-jangle with every move,
Dancing joy, it's all in the groove!

Ninety-nine cents for a dozen, who knew?
They cheer me up when I'm feeling blue.
Swapped them with friends like trading cards,
A fashion statement that's so avant-garde!

So here's to my silly wrist parade,
My laughter-gems never seem to fade.
Let others wear diamonds, that's not my way,
With joyful jewelry, I seize the day!

Links of Legacy

Oh, can you see my linky chains?
Made of noodles and some rubber gains.
They say 'one's trash is another's treasure',
But this is art, beyond all measure!

I stack them high, a rainbow tower,
Each color bright, giving me power.
Tied together with giggles galore,
Just wait till I wear even more!

My grandma said, 'Be wise, my dear.'
'Invest in good stuff, hold it near.'
But here I stand, like a fashion fool,
Wearing these links as my style rule!

With every twist, a story to tell,
Who knew rubber made a life so swell?
In every link, joy's legacy stays,
My noodle bracelet forever sways!

Faithful Fabric

My fabric square, it's quite a sight,
Stitched with laughter, it feels just right.
A patch from here, a patch from there,
It tells a tale, if you just care!

Some call it chaos, I call it art,
Each thread woven straight from the heart.
Colors clash like a wild debate,
But it brings me joy that's first-rate!

Wrapped around my wrist so snug,
It's more than fabric, it's a big hug.
Sometimes it frays, a silly thing,
But each little snag makes my heart sing!

So here's my tale of faithful thread,
Who knew fabric could bring such dread?
Yet, on my wrist, it still will stay,
My funny patchwork leads the way!

Threads of Trust

With these threads, my secrets bind,
A little wacky, more fun to find.
Each knot a promise, a giggling bond,
In this silly game, of which we're fond.

Twisting and turning, we laugh and play,
In a world so wild, we find our way.
I share my snacks, you give me cheer,
Every lonely moment, you mend with beer!

On tangled days, we hold on tight,
The fabric of friendship feels so right.
Through ups and downs, we will not rust,
With every thread, a bit of trust!

So here we stand, just hand in hand,
Making memories, oh isn't it grand?
With threads of laughter, we'll never part,
Together forever, woven from the heart!

Adornments of Aspiration

On my wrist, a rainbow twist,
Each color a little wish.
When I slip, it's quite the trip,
But laughter is my favorite dish.

With charms that jingle, dance in glee,
They cheer me on, like a cup of tea.
Sometimes they tangle, oh what a mess,
Yet they remind me, life's a funny dress.

A purple bead for my sleepy time,
A green one sings, "You're doing fine!"
I wear them proudly, like armor bright,
Armored in chuckles, running through the night.

So here's a cheer for each silly sway,
Fashioned with hope in a playful way.
Adorn yourself with joy and fun,
Life's better danced under the sun.

Harmony in Every Loop

Loop-de-loop on my arm today,
Bright hues spinning, come what may.
They say it's fashion, I just grin,
Feels like wearing laughter from within.

A swish and a sway, they gleefully chime,
With every giggle, they're feeling sublime.
Wobbling about, causing a ruckus,
These colorful bands, oh what a circus!

When I'm feeling down, they jump to the test,
A wristful of joy, 'cause they know what's best.
Each loop a reminder, to giggle and play,
Joy-filled warriors for every day.

So wear your colors, let your spirits soar,
These funny adornments are never a bore.
With each little jingle, life's never a frown,
Harmony plays, spinning round and round.

Hope's Embrace

On my wrist sits snug a band of cheer,
It whispers softly, "Don't you fear!"
When blues align, it gives me a nudge,
"Leap with laughter, don't hold a grudge!"

Wrapped in colors, I'm ready to bloom,
Each twist a giggle, banishing gloom.
When I shake my fist, they shudder in thrill,
"Quirky and bright, let's go for a spill!"

Every pat and poke brings a chuckling tune,
These silly charms dance 'neath the moon.
With each little shimmer, I twirl back in,
Hope finds its rhythm in a joyful spin.

So if you're in need of a funny embrace,
Slip on a band, it's a whimsical race.
Together we'll giggle, and chase away sighs,
With a sprinkle of humor, we'll reach for the skies.

Symbols of Strength

On my wrist, bright symbols align,
They wink and nod, oh aren't they fine?
With a flick and a flip, they shout with glee,
"Stronger together, just wait and see!"

A stretchy charm, a whimsical thing,
Bouncing with hope, like a songbird in spring.
When I'm feeling wobbly, they hang around,
Ready to lift me up off the ground.

Each little bead tells a tale of cheer,
They giggle together, just like good friends here.
In moments of doubt, they twirl with flair,
Whispering, "Dunk your worries, we dare!"

So here's to the bands that rally our heart,
With strength in their colors, they play a part.
Life's a grand circus, step in the ring,
With these symbols of strength, let laughter sing!

Signals of Solidarity

In the crowd, we wave our hands,
Each color brighter than the bands.
We cheer for each other, full of glee,
Like a parade of laughs, come join the spree!

A pink one for smiles, yellow for fights,
Our outfit's a riot, a dazzling sight.
With goofy grins and silly flair,
Unity's wacky, beyond compare!

So tie them tight, let them shine,
With mismatched socks, we redefine.
Together we jive, in this vibrant plot,
Who knew solidarity could be this hot?

Raise a toast, to the looped and the free,
To mismatched colors, 'tween you and me.
Life's a joke, so let's jest,
In our colorful chaos, we are blessed!

Fragments of Faith

With every twist and every turn,
We wear our quirks, it's how we learn.
A splash of green, a dash of gold,
Crafting smiles, like stories told!

Each thread a giggle, each knot a cheer,
In this wacky world, there's nothing to fear.
With clashing patterns, we spin and sway,
Who says fashion can't have a play?

Through ups and downs, what do we find?
Laughter's the secret that all unwind.
In our oddball tale, together we stand,
Like a band of misfits, hand in hand!

From soup to nuts, we ride this life,
Cutting through chaos like a butter knife.
So wear it proudly, let your colors beam,
In our goofy garden, we'll always dream!

Tokens of Triumph

In a world so wild, we laugh and connect,
Each little trinket, a joyful effect.
A nod to success, with every beat,
Despite the odds, we dance on our feet!

Every shade we wear tells a tale,
Of mishaps and laughs, we will prevail.
Like confetti in chaos, we sprinkle the ground,
In the circus of life, we all are profound!

A splash of purple for moments of fun,
Crazy outfits, like it's Halloween done!
With laughter as armor, we conquer our fears,
A festival of friendship, full of cheers!

So here's to the colors that shine with a grin,
In the great game of life, let the fun begin!
Each token we hold, a reminder, you see,
That triumph is best done wackily!

Colors of Community

A rainbow's embrace in our quirky team,
No need for a plan, just let it stream.
With every shade, our spirits align,
Together in laughter, we brightly shine!

From polka dots to stripes, we wear them with flair,
In a kaleidoscope dream, we float through the air.
Each thread binds us tighter, each smile intertwines,
In our vibrant circus, look how it shines!

We juggle our dreams with a twist and a twirl,
With every adventure, watch our hearts whirl.
In our colorful tapestry, we find our way,
In this zany journey, let's laugh and play!

So sip on your coffee, and let's paint the town,
With giggles and cheers, we'll never frown.
In the colors of unity, let's make a stand,
Life's more fun when we all lend a hand!

Woven Whispers

In colors bright, they dance and play,
A fashion choice, in a silly way.
Each twist and turn a story unfolds,
Of laughter shared and secrets told.

With every pull, they stretch and bend,
A quirky accessory, perfect for a friend.
They jingle and jangle, a playful sound,
A reminder of joy that's always around.

They're not just threads, oh no, indeed!
They hold the giggles of every need.
Like silly rubber bands around the wrist,
A funny little gift, how could we resist?

So wear them high, let spirits soar,
A rainbow of vibes, who could ask for more?
In a world that spins, let humor reign,
These woven tales will always entertain.

Shields of Sanctuary

In a clash of colors, we stand so strong,
With silly bracelets, we can do no wrong.
They guard our dreams, or so we say,
While we trip over our own feet, play by play.

Like a fortress built by the hands of friends,
Defending us from the world that pretends.
With goofy charms and patterns galore,
They keep out the blues, and open the door.

Bouncing around, the laughter ignites,
As we wear our shields in the silliest sights.
In this fashion war, there's nothing to fear,
For each wrist will sparkle, bringing good cheer.

So gather your pals, let's layer them on,
In this sanctuary, we can't go wrong.
With a wink and a grin, we'll dance through the day,
In our quirky garb, come what may.

Symbols of Strength

A twist of fate on our colorful bands,
We pull them tight with laughter in hands.
Like superheroes, we strike a pose,
In these silly symbols, our courage grows.

When life gets tough, we giggle and grin,
These funny bracelets just draw us in.
With every pop and bounce, we find our voice,
In humor and fun, we always rejoice.

Tangled together like socks from the wash,
These vibrant loops, the ultimate posh.
They don't fight battles but offer support,
With smiles so bright, we make life a sport.

So wear them proudly, let your heart sing,
For each little thread is a magical thing.
Together we stand, no matter the test,
With symbols that shine, we're truly blessed.

Patterns of Perseverance

In a swirl of hues, we face the day,
With bands of laughter along the way.
Each pop and twist, a giggle awaits,
As we strut through life, embracing our fates.

Like quirky patterns sewn into our souls,
They guide us through, and keep us whole.
These vibrant threads in the silliest shapes,
Remind us to smile when the world escapes.

As we trip and tumble, we just bounce back,
With memories woven into every crack.
Hold tight these charms, in joyous parade,
For every odd moment, a memory made.

So grab your friends, let's wear them with pride,
In this colorful world, we'll nothing to hide.
Through struggles and laughter, we'll march on ahead,
With laughter as armor, our spirits widespread.

Marks of a Mission

In every color, stories told,
A rainbow arm, quite bold!
They wobble when I jump and run,
Like silly bands, oh what fun!

Each one a charm, a friendly lure,
For folks who giggle, that's for sure.
They stretch and bounce, a playful sight,
Making every day feel light!

Wrap them tight, then dance around,
In goofy moves, joy is found.
While sharing laughs, we twirl and spin,
Mark my words, let the fun begin!

So gather 'round, let's make a show,
With bands aplenty, we steal the glow!
We'll spark a riot of silly cheer,
With every twist, we conquer fear!

Armbands of Alliance

Together we stand, in bright displays,
Armbands sparkling in sunny rays.
A mismatched bunch, with tales to spin,
Unite us all, let the laughter begin!

When skies are gray, we won't despair,
Our colorful ties will comb the hair!
Each band a buddy, oh what a crew,
In our zany world, we find what's true!

Arm in arm, we prance and play,
With bouncy steps, hip-hip-hooray!
They flail about as we run and leap,
In this joyful ride, we'll never sleep!

So here's our oath, with laughter we blend,
These bands of joy, they never end.
In every twist, a giggle awaits,
Alliance forged with playful fates!

Collective Colors

A jumbled bunch, like jelly beans,
We strut our stuff in wacky scenes!
Each hue a giggle, a cheerful grin,
Collective joy, let the fun begin!

From neon greens to quiet blues,
These colors dance like playful shoes.
Together we shine, a vibrant crew,
Creating mischief, and laughter too!

In circle games we trip and fall,
With loud giggles that echo the hall.
Let's paint the day with silly sprays,
In wacky worlds, our laughter stays!

So grab your mates, join in the sway,
With colors bright, we'll seize the day!
Collector's dream of joy and cheer,
In every twist, our friendship's clear!

Bracelets of Belief

Worn upon each wrist, they cling tight,
With stories woven, a playful sight.
Each bead a wish, a ticklish dance,
In ridiculous moments, we take a chance!

Through tickles and giggles, we find our way,
As we bounce about, and foolishly sway.
These bands of hope, in laughter we trust,
With zany dreams, it's a must!

Like party hats for hands, we laugh and play,
Sprinkling sunshine along the way.
With every jingle, a tickle of glee,
Our joyful hearts, forever free!

So clasp them on, let's dance in style,
With bands of belief that make us smile!
In every jostle, our spirits soar,
Together we shout, "Let's dance some more!"

Signs of Survival

In a world that's sometimes wild,
We wear these bands, quite beguiled.
Colors bright and shapes so neat,
A fashion statement, can't be beat!

They tell a tale of laughter loud,
With every twist, we feel quite proud.
In times of strife, we wave and cheer,
These little loops—our badge to wear!

A purple one for tea at noon,
A polka dot for dancing soon.
In each knot, a giggle grows,
Like silly socks, they steal the show!

So here's to bands that give us glee,
We strut around like it's day three.
Survival's got a quirky flair,
We'll laugh 'til our band gets wear and tear!

Awakened Anchors

From deep slumber, we arise,
With vibrant hues to catch the eyes.
These little loops, our charm so sweet,
Like rubber ducks, they can't be beat!

They bounce around with every move,
While keeping us in our funky groove.
With every shake, they sing a tune,
Like jolly frogs beneath the moon.

One's got stripes, another's plain,
Together they dance through joy and pain.
An anchor here, a joy to hold,
And never once do they get old!

Awake, alive, we twirl about,
In these bands, we scream and shout.
Our hearts are light, we sway and swing,
With joy and laughter, we embrace spring!

Unity in Colors

Oh look at us, a rainbow crew,
With colors bright, all fresh and new.
A twist of fate, a wacky sight,
We mingle 'round, it feels so right!

Together we dance, a sight to see,
Our bands all jingle, like jubilee.
In every hue, a story's spun,
Who knew the fun had just begun?

Some are vivid, others calm,
They wrap us tight, like a soothing balm.
In the crowd, we strut with cheer,
Each band a hug that draws us near!

With every friendship that we make,
These bands of joy, we won't forsake.
In every chuckle, in every sway,
Our colors shine, come laugh and play!

Adornments of Ascent

Climbing high, we reach for stars,
With funky bands as our memoirs.
A tiny leap, a little bound,
With silly looks, we're glory-bound!

These bands are badges of delight,
Like jellybeans, they're a pure bite.
When we fall, we laugh instead,
With colors bright, we forge ahead!

From thrift shop finds to crafty dreams,
An artful mess, or so it seems.
They twirled around our weary wrists,
With every twist, we shake off lists!

So raise a cheer for every match,
In each of us, let's find a catch.
Ascent awaits with every smile,
In bands of joy, we'll walk a mile!